Zhiyan Cheng's Batik & Silk Paintings
程之彦蜡染与绸画

by Hsiaoling Cheng
程小玲

FRONT COVER:
Detail from the Horse, 1988
Batik on velvet, 84x70cm

BACK COVER:
Birds, 1990
Watercolor on silk, 36x22cm

FRONTISPIECE:
Silk Road, 1990
Batik on velvet, 102x82cm

Photo: Zhiyan Cheng, 1978

Published by: New Arts

封面：唐三彩，1988
彩色蜡染，天鹅绒布 84x70cm
封底：鸟，1990
水彩，36x22cm
插图：丝绸之路，1990
彩色蜡染 102x82cm

画家照片：程之彦，1978

新艺术出版社

www.batik-painting.com
ISBN: 978-1-4243-3712-5

Acknowledgments
致谢

I would like to acknowledge the enormous assistance given to me while making *Zhiyan Cheng's Batik & Silk Paintings* a reality. I am grateful to my father's sister, Professor Shunying, who carefully read and edited my Chinese manuscript; my father's schoolmates and friends, Yanbin Li and Professor Zhicheng Lao, who wrote the commentary for this book; Bruce Rapp, Patricia Borre and Ruth Banagan for their contribution in editing the English version, and a special thanks to Louis Lok, who instructed me on how to create an art book layout. Most of all, I want to thank George Zhou and Royes Lo, who taught me the techniques involved in how to edit images to meet standard requirements for the press.

在此，我要感谢所有的亲人和朋友们为编辑和出版《程之彦蜡染与绸画》所给予的帮助。感谢姑母程舜英教授，她不但亲自撰文纪念家父，还对这本画册的中文文字进行了精心修改。感谢家父早年的同学及生前好友李彦彬先生、老志诚教授为画册题词。感谢Bruce Rapp先生、Patricia Borre 女士、Ruth Banagan女士，他们花了大量的时间对画册的英文文字做了修订。我还要感谢 Louis Lok 先生，他指导我如何编辑画册。而且，我要特别感谢周季先生、Royes Lo先生，是他们教会我图像处理的方法，从而使画册中的图像达到印刷标准。

Dedicated to My Father, Zhiyan Cheng

献给敬爱的父亲

程之彦

1918 - 2001

Contents

目录

Introduction 7
程之彦蜡染与绸画介绍

Batiks 12
蜡染作品

Silk Paintings 44
绸画作品

Epilogue 70
后记

Introduction

Zhiyan Cheng's Batik and Silk Paintings

Zhiyan Cheng's textile paintings are so richly colored and beautiful that people who have viewed his artistic creations for the first time, find his artwork to be incredible, because his paintings were not painted; they were hand-dyed.

Cheng studied traditional Chinese painting when he was a child. At college, he majored in industrial arts. He was very skilled at Chinese ink and wash, oil painting, watercolor, and sculpture. However, what he loved doing the most was the traditional Chinese handmade batik.

Traditional Chinese batik belongs in the craft category. The craftsman paints a pattern on the cloth and the unpainted areas are coated with wax. After dyeing and removing wax, the cloth shows a white background with colored patterns. The color bleeds through the wax and creates a natural crackling design. Chinese batik was mainly used for clothing and accessories.

Cheng possessed a keen sense of perception and imagination. He discovered that although Chinese batik had simple patterns with monotone coloring, its natural cracklings made it a unique artistic idiom. This led to incredibly attractive patterns in the painting, resembling ripples on a lake, clouds in the sky, or veined marble. These varied crackling patterns could evoke innumerable, imaginative responses in the viewers.

Cheng's goal was to create a brand new art form by adapting Western drawing skills to watercolor and oil paintings, as well as Chinese ink and wash on cloth. Using Chinese batik dye method to formulate the colors was part of the process. Cheng began to develop his idea of combining painting and dyeing when he was in college. He held two solo batik art shows in Beijing in 1941 and 1942. These shows resulted in a wave of enthusiastic approval throughout the art circles. Cheng elevated batik from a handmade craft to a new, highly elegant, fine art platform.

Dye colors commonly used in traditional Chinese batik, are dark blue, bright red, light yellow and greenish blue. The dyeing method is simple; the colors do not show layers or depth. Since

Cheng desired his batiks to achieve the same results as that of watercolor and oil paintings, he had to use complex painting techniques. His greatest challenge however, was to chemically invent new dye colors and to discover an entirely new method of dyeing.

Many kinds of dye pigments existed; Cheng constantly thought about which materials would produce the best results. His home was transformed from an artist's studio to a chemical laboratory. It was littered with chemical dyes and lab equipment. He collected as many dye pigments as he could and invested countless hours examining the brightness and saturation qualities of each. He also tested the durability of the colors on the various textiles. If the colors on the fabric did not debilitate after exposure to sunlight and soap wash, the batik artwork was worthy to be part of a collection. Ultimately, Cheng selected a vast variety of colors, which remained constant and durable after the textile dyeing procedures.

Paints and dyes are very different in their application. In oil or watercolor painting, the color used by the artist is the hue that shows on the painting. With dyes, however, the dye color usually appears differently after the application. For example, the green dye will show up later as a dark purple, and brown dyes will appear as grey. Furthermore, dyes, which are initially all water-clear before application, ultimately create the red, blue, and grey colors after application, thus, the artist cannot perceive the final color while painting with the dye colors and this is the most challenging part of the process. Cheng's vast knowledge regarding textiles and dyes made him a master of dyeing skills.

The most important artistic aspect of Cheng's batiks was the variety of his subjects. He could paint scenery, animals, still life, figures and more, without having the limitation of the traditional Chinese batik pattern forms. Cheng's other improved method was to adopt the Chinese ink and wash painting technique for use on batiks. Although Chinese ink and wash had only one color, variety was featured through its various shadowing and shadings. This allowed the batik to appear complex thus, inviting the viewer to venture into the depths of Cheng's designs to absorb the greater details. It is a travesty that most of Cheng's single color, ink and wash batiks have been lost and therefore cannot be shown in this book.

Another of Cheng's achievements was his silk painting. He was able to express his artistic abilities by incorporating both his paint and dye methods on silk, much better than on paper. Cheng's silk paintings pursued a natural, lifelike idiom, and reflected the traditional Chinese ink and wash artistic concept. To blend his art motifs, Cheng elected to paint on selected silks. The natural textured patterns of the silk enhanced the painting, adding depth, detail and reality to his designs. He used different painting styles based on the painting motifs. With all of these techniques combined, Zhiyan Cheng created his own silk painting style.

This book represents only a part of Zhiyan Cheng's collection of batik and silk paintings. Cheng produced many beautiful batiks during the 1940's; but most of them have been lost. Cheng's family was impoverished at the time; his cloth batiks were used as bed sheets or pillowcases. Everything that was not used was sold. The few masterpieces, which he retained in his collection, did not survive the artistic holocaust of the Great Cultural Revolution in China. Most of the batik paintings in this book were produced after Cheng retired in 1988.

In Zhiyan Cheng's diary, he once commented, "Fine art is not commonly seen in the creation of batiks, because it calls for craftsmen and artists who are skillful and knowledgeable both in painting and dyeing techniques. Through my experimentation, my work alone shows that it is possible."

程之彦的蜡染艺术与绸画介绍

一幅幅精美、绚丽的绘画作品，竟然是用手工蜡染的技法绘制出来的，简直令人难以置信。几乎所有看过程之彦蜡染作品的人都会发出这样的感叹。

程之彦自幼学习中国山水花鸟画。在大学期间主修西方工艺美术。他的艺术爱好十分广泛，中国画、油画、水彩画和雕塑他都很精通。而最让他着迷的是中国的传统蜡染。

中国传统蜡染，是用蜡刀蘸熔蜡绘花于布，然后再用蓝靛浸染，染后去蜡，布面就呈现出白底蓝花的多种图案。中国传统蜡染主要用于制作服装、服饰和各种生活实用品。

程之彦对周围的事物敏感且想象丰富。他发现中国传统蜡染中蕴含着一种独特的艺术表现力。在染色时，染料顺着蜡片碎裂后形成的裂纹渗到布面上，留下了形态各异的纹理，就好似湖海的波纹、天上的浮云和岩石上的花纹一样，呈现出一幅浑然天成的自然图画，给人带来无限的遐想。

程之彦对蜡染产生兴趣的真正原因，是要创造出一种全新的蜡染艺术。他希望能够用中国蜡染的方法染出西方油画、水彩画和中国水墨画那样的美术作品。大学期间，他就开始尝试先在棉布上直接绘画，然后用蜡染的技法着色。他于 1941 和 1942 年两届在北京举行个人蜡染画展，表现题材一举突破了传统蜡染所沿用了数百年的花边和图案形式，令人耳目一新，在当时的美术界产生了很大反响。评论说，程之彦的蜡染作品把民间传统手工艺术带进了高雅的艺术殿堂。

采用传统蜡染技法来表现绘画作品，最大的挑战是染色。中国传统蜡染常用的染料有藏青、朱红、鹅黄、淡青等少数几种。染色的方法一般是单色平染，颜色单调且缺乏层次感。如果想使蜡染达到油画或水彩画的艺术表现力，就必须尝试新的染料和染色方法。

世界上的染料品种很多，究竟使用哪种染料绘画可以达到最佳效果则成了程之彦日夜琢磨的事情。他的居室由画室变成了化学试验室，各种化学染料和实验器皿摆满了房间。他收集了当时所有能得到的染料并细心地研究和挑选。蜡染色彩的形成不仅取决于颜色的色调，还取决于颜色的亮度和饱和度。为了掌握染料的实际色彩效果，他对每一种染料都要多次试染、反复尝试。这样形成的染色样品和染色时的物理、化学条件就成为他以后蜡染绘画的“调色板”。在筛选染料时，他不仅考虑色彩，还考虑颜色的稳定性和染料对画布有无腐蚀作用。只有当一幅画染色完成后，其颜色能长时间的稳定不变，且经得起水洗日晒，它才可能成为有收藏价值的作品。程之彦选中的染料大多数属于活性还原染料，这类染料的优点是色彩丰富，染成的作品颜色亮丽而持久。

在着色方面，使用染料绘画与使用颜料绘画有很大的不同。在绘制油画或水彩画时，画家把颜料调成什么颜色，它在画中就显示出什么颜色。而使用染料绘画着色时，则包含上色和显色两个步骤。很多染料在显色前后呈现的颜色是不一样的。例如：绿色染料的颜色在显色之前呈酱紫色；棕色呈浅灰色；而红、蓝、灰居然是无色的。在绘画时画家不能当时看到最终的颜色，这正是用染料绘画的最难之处。经过长期对染料的潜心研究，再加上程之彦对纺织品及染色技法的丰富经验，使得他在蜡染着色方面达到了驾轻就熟的地步。

题材广泛是程之彦蜡染绘画的另一个显著特点。他摆脱了传统蜡染的局限，尽情地表现自然风景、动物、静物、人物等题材。他将中国画的绘画方法融入蜡染制作也是一个创新。他认为，虽然水墨画是单色，但也有色彩元素，即墨色的明暗度。以水墨画法绘制成的单色蜡染笔触效果强， 表现技巧复杂， 层次丰富。可惜的是他的单色蜡染绘画作品所剩无几。

丝绸绘画是程之彦艺术生涯中的又一个亮点。对熟悉纺织品和印染的程之彦来说，在丝绸上绘画比在纸上绘画可以有更大的表现空间。他既可以使用染色的方法，也可以使用颜料的方法着色。程之彦的丝绸画追求的是一种形神兼备的境界，他善于利用丝绸提花纺织出来的图案纹理，来丰富绘画的层次和表现景物的真实感。他的作品既体现了中国画的“意境”理念，又不拘泥传统国画的常规模式和套路，绘画手法因题材而变, 使得他的丝绸绘画呈现出了自己特有的风格。

本画册收集了程之彦的部分蜡染和丝绸绘画作品。在四十年代，他绘制了较多的蜡染作品。由于那时家中生活贫困，其中的大部分被卖掉或家用；余下的部分在文化大革命动乱时期也未能幸免。在这本画册中所展示的蜡染和丝绸绘画作品，多是程之彦在 1988 年退休以后绘制的。

在日记中程之彦曾这样评价自己：“在蜡染领域，表现绘画艺术的作品还很少见。它需要染色技术和绘画艺术的结合，我就是做这种尝试的人。”

Batiks

蜡染作品

Sapphire Dragon 1988, Batik on velvet 80x60cm 龙

Silk Road 1990, Batik on velvet 102x82cm
丝绸之路

Blue Heron 1989, Batik on velvet 65x84cm
苍鹭

Blue Heron 1989, Batik on velvet 65x84cm
苍鹭

Still Life 1988, Batik on velvet 62x82cm 静物

Crescent Oasis 1988, Batik on velvet 84x64cm 月牙泉

Zebras 1989, Batik on velvet 82x82cm 斑马

Tiger 1988, Batik on velvet 98x82cm 虎

Detail from **The Great Wall of China** 长城 细部

The Great Wall of China 1990, Batik on velvet 64x84cm 长城

Crouching Tiger 1989, Batik on velvet 65x84cm 卧虎

Tropical Fish 1988, Batik on velvet 65x55cm 热带鱼

Detail from **Horse** 唐三彩 细部

Horse - Tang Dynasty three-color pottery 1988, Batik on velvet 84x70cm 马－唐三彩

Details from **Vase and Roses** 花瓶、玫瑰花 细部

Vase and Roses 1988, Batik on velvet 42x68xcm 花瓶、玫瑰花

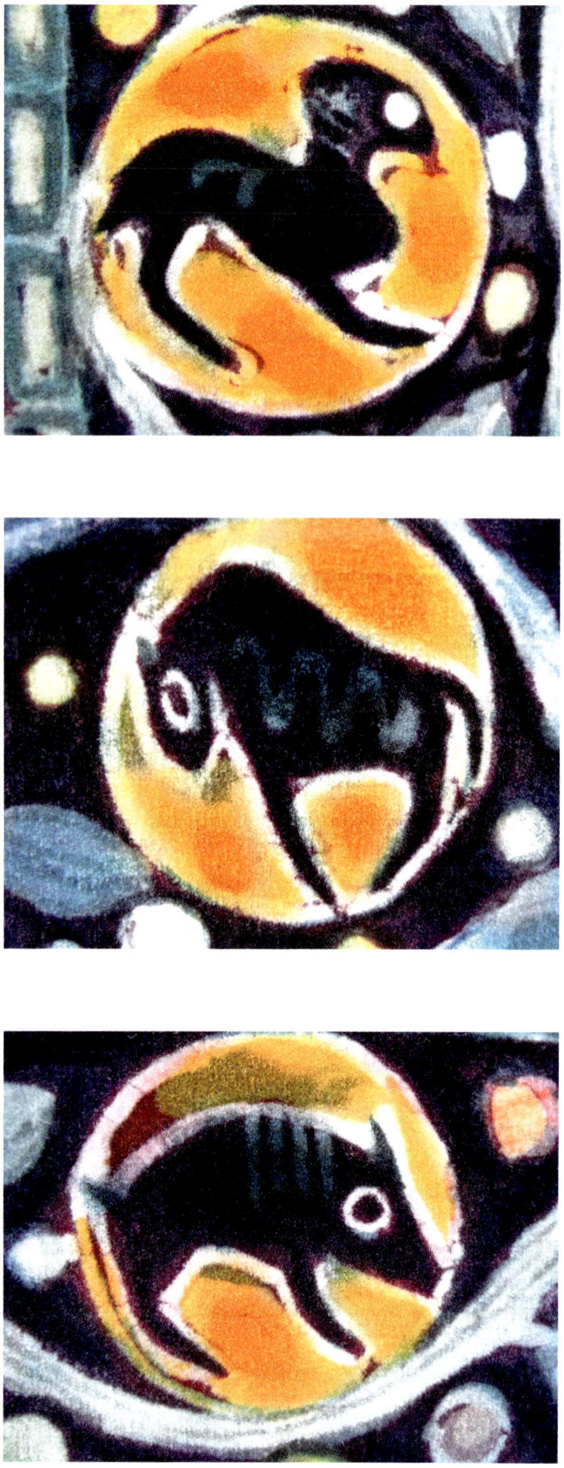

Animals 1988, Batik on velvet 12x10cm 动物

Ox Cart (tomb figure for emperors) 1988, Batik on velvet 84x70cm 牛车－唐三彩

The Skilled Pi-pa Player (Pi-pa: Stringed instrument) 1990, Batik on velvet 82x147cm
反弹琵琶

Details from **The Skilled Pi-pa Player** 反弹琵琶 细部

Borders Batik on velvet 花边

Dragon in the Sky 1939, Batik on velvet 48x50cm 彩龙

Detail from **Four Sheep** Door Curtain
四羊 门帘细部

Four Sheep Door Curtain 1938,
Batik on casual cotton 78x170cm 四羊门帘

Five Sparrows 1941, Batik on velvet 82x70cm (Won Best in Show, Beijing, 1944)
五雀图(曾获北京美术节特奖, 1944 年)

Details from **Five Sparrows** shown on page 41 五雀图 细部

Details from **Five Sparrows** shown on page 41 五雀图 细部

Silk Paintings

绸画作品

Cat 1992, Watercolor on jacquard (textured) silk 28x36cm 猫

Fish 1992, Watercolor on textured silk 29x19.5cm 鱼

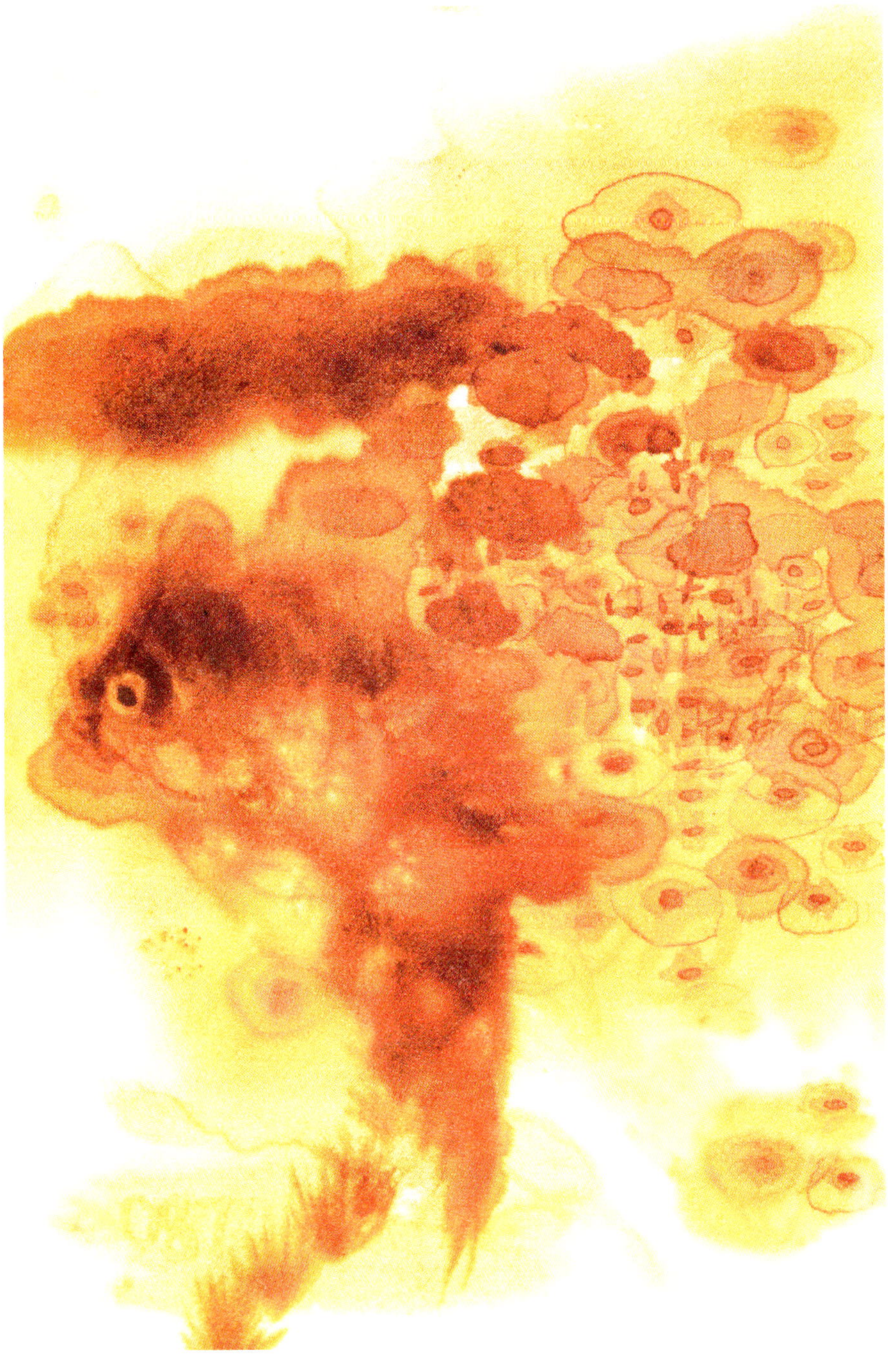

Gold Fish in Pond 1994, Watercolor on silk 14x20cm 池塘中的金鱼

Chasing Fish 1990, Watercolor on silk 13x22cm 追鱼

Frog 1988, Watercolor on silk 18x26cm 塘蛙

Cranes 1988, Watercolor on silk 20x29cm 鹤

Humming Birds 1989, Watercolor on textured silk 18x23cm 翠鸟

Birds 1995, Watercolor on textured silk 16x26cm 双鸟

Birds 1990, Watercolor on textured silk 29x18cm 枝头

Dragonfly 1990, Watercolor on textured silk 17.5x18cm 蜻蜓

Ducks 1989, Watercolor on textured silk 13x21cm 鸭

Butterfly and Wisteria 1990, Watercolor on textured silk 19x27cm 藤萝与蝴蝶

Hen and Rooster 1991, Watercolor on textured silk 25x18cm 鸡

Staring 1994, Watercolor on crepe silk 40x36cm 窥

Zebras 1988, Watercolor on textured silk 48x38 斑马

Bird Resting on Lotus 1988, Ink and color wash on silk 24x35cm 荷花

Flowers 1996, Acrylic on tie-dye silk 44x28cm **花** 扎染

Birds on the White Cherry Blossom 1995, Watercolor on textured silk 32x28cm 鸟与梅花

Waterfall and Mist 1989, Watercolor on crepe silk 36x46cm 雾中瀑布

Tree 1994 , Watercolor on textured silk 20x28cm 树

Sunset 1994 , Watercolor on textured silk 28x20cm 晚霞

Mountain 1988, Watercolor on silk 28x32cm 山

Oasis 1988, Watercolor on silk 32x28cm 月牙泉

Crystal Waterfall 1993, Watercolor on textured silk 20x28cm 瀑布

Pagoda 1993, Watercolor on textured silk 28x12cm 塔

Epilogue

后记

Zhiyan Cheng's Life and His Arts

My father, Zhiyan Cheng, was born in Beijing in 1918. His father, Shude Cheng, studied law in Japan, published many books about the history of Chinese laws and was a famous law scholar in China. His mother, Timin Shen, was the first female scholar to graduate from Fu-Jian Women's Normal School.

My father was gifted, and attracted to painting from the time he was a child. He majored in industrial arts in Beijing Normal University. Under the guidance of his famous teachers and motivated by his own talent and diligence, he was able to adopt the best techniques from each of his masters and create his own. When he was 20 years old, he started painting on textiles. In 1941 and 1942, he organized two solo batik shows, exhibiting his portfolio of unique painting and dyeing techniques. His creative batik paintings were well received by the art circles and he became quite famous when he was young.

After graduating from college, he became a middle school art teacher. Later, he worked in Beijing Fine Art College as Chief of the Batik Department. Beginning in 1954, he worked as a senior textile engineer and senior silk specialist for China Silk Corp. and China Silk Import & Export Corp. He visited many countries throughout the world. Based on his studies and research, he improved silk quality and silk dyeing and weaving techniques. He published many books and articles about silk. In 1994, *China International Famous Person Press* recorded him on the list of well-known persons who made great contributions to the silk industry.

Upon his retirement in 1988, he started to paint batik again after a 40 year hiatus. The first problem to surmount was to convert his one bedroom apartment into a studio. There he completed the full batik dyeing process - designing, painting, waxing, coloring, boiling, rinsing and drying. Dyeing required numerous consecutive steps. He could not stop in the middle of the process and often spent ten hours to complete one dyeing cycle. Much of the time he was exposed to irritating chemical agents and strong light, surrounded by hot equipment and pots of boiling water. He put in tremendously hard work, both mental and physical, to finish one piece of batik painting.

My father devoted himself to his art and created more than 20 batik paintings within three years. In the winter of 1988, he wrote a letter to me describing his feeling: "While I was in college, I ran a solo batik show every year. After graduation, I had no chance or time to paint for more than 40 years. Now I am 71 years old and retired, I have started to paint again. I couldn't believe that my painting skills have not completely dried up; my artwork still arouses appreciation and enjoyment in people. I feel as if I was born again. Whenever I think of or see some of my favorite paintings, my first feeling is that I have returned to the interests of my youth. I am very excited and feel that my life is abundant. This kind of enjoyment and satisfaction cannot be materially measured."

In addition to painting and dyeing batik, he also painted on silk. His silk paintings were serene, peaceful, and captured every detail of nature. He chose to paint on selected silks with the appropriate background patterns, which together made his silk paintings more beautiful and expressive. His silk paintings won many awards and prizes. His first art show was at Kenilworth, New Jersey in 1988; his painting of two roosters won first place in the watercolor category. In 1995, his painting of four flying birds won best in show among 40 artists in the Plainfield annual art festival. From 1988 to 2001, his treasured silk paintings were proudly featured in more than 40 art shows on the East Coast of the United States. He won eight first place prizes and other notable awards.

My father passed away in 2001. He planned to publish his batik artwork when he was alive. To make my father's wish come true, and allow more people appreciate his special area of creative art, my brothers, sister and I have spent over two years compiling my father's papers, diaries and letters related to his artwork. We also visited my father's old classmates and former friends to get information on my father's school life, important occasions and solo shows. Based on the collected information and suggestions, we took pictures of all the batiks we could find and designed the art book. Finally my father's art book is finished.

I dedicate the publication of *Zhiyan Cheng's Batik & Silk Paintings* to honor my loving father, may his soul rest in peace.

记父亲程之彦

我的父亲程之彦生于1918年，福建闽侯人，出身书香门第。祖父程树德，清末进士，日本政法大学毕业；曾任北京大学、清华大学法学教授；著有《九朝律考》、《论语注释》等书，是我国早期法律界著名学者。祖母沈缇珉，是福建女子师范学校第一届毕业生。

家父天生聪慧好学，从小就显示出绘画的天赋。1938年，他考入北京师范大学工艺系，攻读工艺美术专业。期间他接受了中国传统画和西方现代绘画的系统美术教育，并得到了蒋兆和、郭柏川、汪慎生、胡佩衡等一些当代著名画家的特别指导，为他的美术技艺打下良好基础，使其天赋得到进一步发展。二十岁时，他就开始尝试把自己独特的绘画艺术风格体现在纺织品上。1941年和1942年，他在北京中山公园"来今雨轩"两次举行个人蜡染画展。由于他突破了传统蜡染形式，将西方绘画技法与中国传统蜡染工艺相结合，绘画及染色手法新颖，题材丰富，获得当时美术界的一致称赞，轰动一时。

大学毕业后，家父先后在北京三中、北京崇德中学任美术教师，并于中央美术学院从事蜡染艺术的研究工作。从1954年开始，家父先后在中国纺织品进出口总公司、中国丝绸公司、中国丝绸进出口总公司担任工程师、高级工程师、高级专家的职务。他代表中国丝绸公司出使世界多个国家，长期致力于绸缎图案、丝绸品种、花色和生产工艺的设计研究。他在报刊杂志上多次发表有关丝绸设计方面的文章，并参与大型学术画册《中国丝绸》的资料收集和编写工作。1994年，家父被列入由中国国际名人院编著的《奉献在丝绸》名人录中，文章称赞他为中国丝绸业的发展做出了杰出贡献。

1988年，家父退休后立即着手恢复他四十年前心爱的蜡染创作。他克服了以居室为画室的种种不便，将设计、绘画、涂蜡、水煮着色等蜡染制作的多道工序全部在他那一间居室内完成；他连续地坚持在强灯光、火炉、沸水和呛鼻的化学染剂下长时间地作业。可以说，他的每一幅蜡染创作，都是他脑力和体力的极大付出。但家父却始终乐此不倦，仅三年中就创作了二十多幅蜡染艺术作品。1988年冬，家父在给我的信中这样描述他当时的心情："我在大学读书时，每年举行一次个人蜡染画展。毕业后，由于工作繁忙而无暇顾及，竟一置四十年。现在我已七十一岁，退休开始再画，居然我的绘画能力还没有全部枯萎，我的绘画作品还有很多人欣赏，此等感觉如同再生，四十年恍如隔世，有一种特殊的安慰感。我每每在想起那些得意之作时，第一个感觉是恢复了年青时的乐趣，同时也欣慰我的光阴没有白白流逝。每当我画出一张好作品时，高兴极了，生活感到充实。这种高兴，不是从物质上可以衡量的。”

退休后，家父除创作蜡染作品外，同时也在丝绸上用颜料绘画。他的绸画体现了世外桃源的意境，画法细腻、用色柔和自然，再衬以丝绸本身的花纹，使他的绸画更加绚丽多姿。他的绸画作品曾在美国画展中多次获奖。1988年，他的绸画首次在美国新泽西州肯尼沃思镇参加画展，就被评为水彩画类第一名。1995年在美国新泽西州普兰费尔德镇一年一度的美术节上，他画的四只飞鸟，在四十多位参展画家中获得全场第一名。自1988年至2001年间，家父的绸画作品在美国东部参加大小型画展共约四十次，获得八次一等奖和多次其它奖项。

家父在世时，一直希望把自己的蜡染作品编辑成画册出版，以让更多的人理解、欣赏他的蜡染创作，并希望能为蜡染艺术的发展做出贡献。家父的愿望我们铭记于心。为了家父的蜡染艺术不致湮没，我们兄弟姐妹用了两年多的时间整理家父的蜡染作品及有关文字、书信，同时还拜访了家父的同学和生前好友，他们提供了家父当年大学学习和举办蜡染展览的情况，并对画册的出版给予了很好的建议。最后再经照相、文字编辑、画册排版设计，这本画册终于得以完成。

我谨以《程之彦蜡染与绸画》画集的问世，告慰家父在天之灵。

Chronology
生平记事

Cheng: a high school student. 1933
中学时期

1918

Zhiyan Cheng is born in Beijing. His mother was the first female scholar to graduate from Fu-Jian Woman's Normal School. She discovered and cultivated Cheng's natural talent for painting from an early age.
程之彦一月十三日出生于北京。母亲沈缇珉是福建女子师范学校第一届毕业生，她早期发现了程之彦的绘画天分。

1925

He teaches himself to draw. He is encouraged by his mother and later, guided by a cousin, who is an artist, Cheng displays his growing mastery of art.
幼时在母亲的引导下，他经常在纸上描绘自己周围的东西。后经懂绘画的表哥指点，渐入正轨。

Cheng's teacher, famous artist, Zhaohe Jiang, painted this portrait of Cheng in 1942.
著名画家蒋兆和祝贺程之彦大学毕业，特为其画像

1938

He pursues the study of industrial arts in Beijing Normal University. He creates his innovative painting styles and techniques on textiles.
考入北京师范大学工艺系，就读工艺美术专业，接受了正规美术教育，艺术天赋得到发展，并开始把自己独特的绘画艺术风格体现在纺织品上。

1941 - 1942

He holds two solo batik shows, exhibiting his unique painting and dyeing techniques. His creative arts

are well received by the art circles and his fame increases.
在北京中山公园“来今雨轩”举行两届个人蜡染画展。他的蜡染创作将西方绘画技法与中国传统蜡染工艺相结合，获得当时美术界的一致称赞，轰动一时。

1946 - 1949
He is an art teacher at the Beijing No.3 Middle School and the Chong-De Middle School.
先后在北京三中，北京崇德中学任美术教师。

1950
At the Beijing Fine Art College, he earns the position as Chief of the Batik Department.
在中央美术学院蜡染部工作，任职蜡染部股长。

1954 - 1987
He works as a senior textile engineer and senior silk specialist for China Silk Corporation and China Silk Import and Export Corporation. During this time, he publishes many books and articles about silk.
先后在中国纺织品进出口总公司、中国丝绸公司、中国丝绸进出口总公司担任高级工程师、高级专家。致力于丝绸品种、花色和生产工艺的设计研究。在报刊杂志上多次发表有关丝绸方面的文章。

1988
He retires from his textile engineering career. After a forty year hiatus, Cheng returns to his artistic passion of dyeing and painting batik, and creates his new collection of silk paintings.
退休后立即着手恢复四十年前心爱的蜡染制作，同时在丝绸上用颜料绘画。

Batik exhibition: Beijing, 1942 - Cheng was 24 years old.
1942 年七月，北京中山公园举办个人蜡染画展 - 时年 24 岁

Photo taken at the batik show of Han Dynasty Stamp.
北京中山公园个人蜡染画展作品：仿汉印

Cheng returned to the show site 36 years later in 1978.
1978 年，三十六年后重回原地拍照

1991

He visits the United States and attends many art shows on the East Coast. Again, his talents are recognized and honored as his silk paintings received many awards and prizes.

旅居美国一年， 在美国东部亲自参加美术画展，绸画作品在画展中多次获奖。

1994

He is honored by *China International Famous Person Press,* in their list of well-known persons who have made great contributions to the silk industry.

被列入由中国国际名人院编著的《奉献在丝绸》名人录，其中称赞程之彦为中国丝绸业发展作出了杰出贡献。

2001

In May, Zhiyan Cheng dies in Beijing, China.

5 月 25 日逝世于北京。

Cheng started to paint batik again after his retirement from textile engineering in 1988.

程之彦七十周岁退休后开始画第一张蜡染。1988 年一月

Cheng organized a silk exhibition in 1982.

1982 年在国外参加中国丝绸展览会。

Cheng gave this piece from his batik artwork to his American friend, Carl Young. November, 1990

程之彦将其蜡染作品赠送给美国友人。1990 年秋

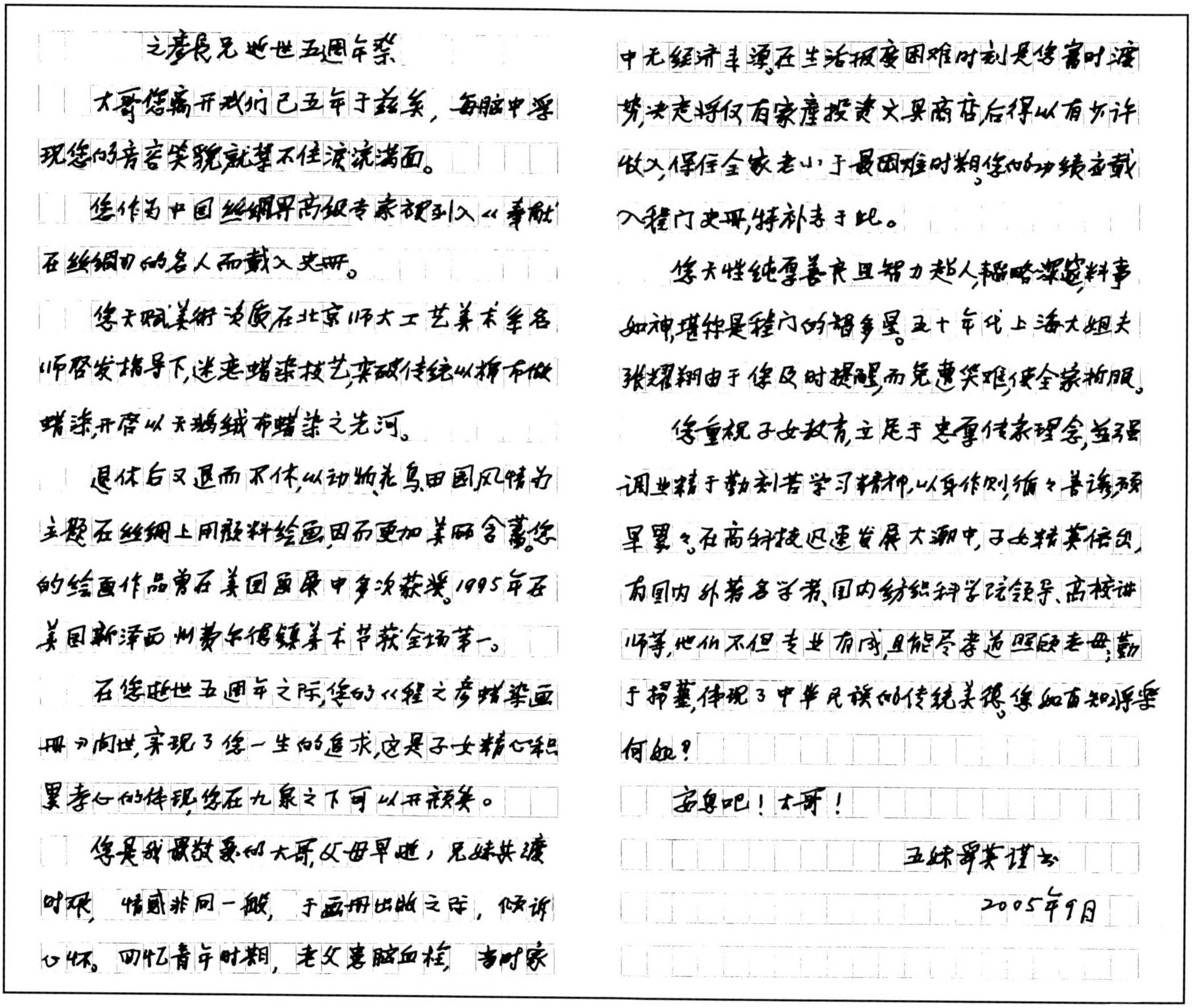

之彦长兄逝世五周年祭

大哥您离开我们已五年于兹矣，每脑中浮现您的音容笑貌就禁不住泪流满面。

您作为中国丝绸界高级专家被列入《奉献在丝绸业的名人》而载入史册。

您天赋美术资质，在北京师大工艺美术系名师启发指导下，迷恋蜡染技艺，突破传统以棉布做蜡染，开启以天鹅绒布蜡染之先河。

退休后又退而不休，以动物、花鸟、田园风情为主题在丝绸上用颜料绘画，因而更加美丽含蓄。您的绘画作品曾在美国画展中多次获奖。1995年在美国新泽西州费尔德镇美术节获全场第一。

在您逝世五周年之际，您的《程之彦蜡染画册》问世，实现了您一生的追求，这是子女精心积累孝心的体现，您在九泉之下可以开颜矣。

您是我最敬爱的大哥，父母早逝，兄妹共渡时艰，情感非同一般，于画册出版之际，倾诉心怀。回忆青年时期，老父患脑血栓，当时家中无经济来源，在生活极度困难时刻是您审时度势，决定将仅有家产投资文具商店，后得以有少许收入，保住全家老小，于最困难时期。您的功绩应载入程门史册，特补书于此。

您天性纯厚善良且智力超人，韬略深邃，料事如神，堪称是程门的智多星。五十年代上海大姐夫张耀翔由于您及时提醒，而免遭灾难，使全家折服。

您重视子女教育，立足于忠厚传家理念，并强调要精于勤、刻苦学习精神，以身作则，循循善诱，硕果累累。在高科技迅速发展大潮中，子女精英倍出，有国内外著名学者、国内纺织科学院领导、高校讲师等，他们不但专业有成，且能尽孝道照顾老母，勤于扫墓，体现了中华民族的传统美德。您如有知将要何如？

安息吧！大哥！

五妹舜英谨书

2005年9月

On the 5th anniversary of Zhiyan Cheng's passing, Professor Shunying Cheng wrote a memorial to his brother.

程之彦逝世五周年之际，程舜英教授撰文纪念他的哥哥。

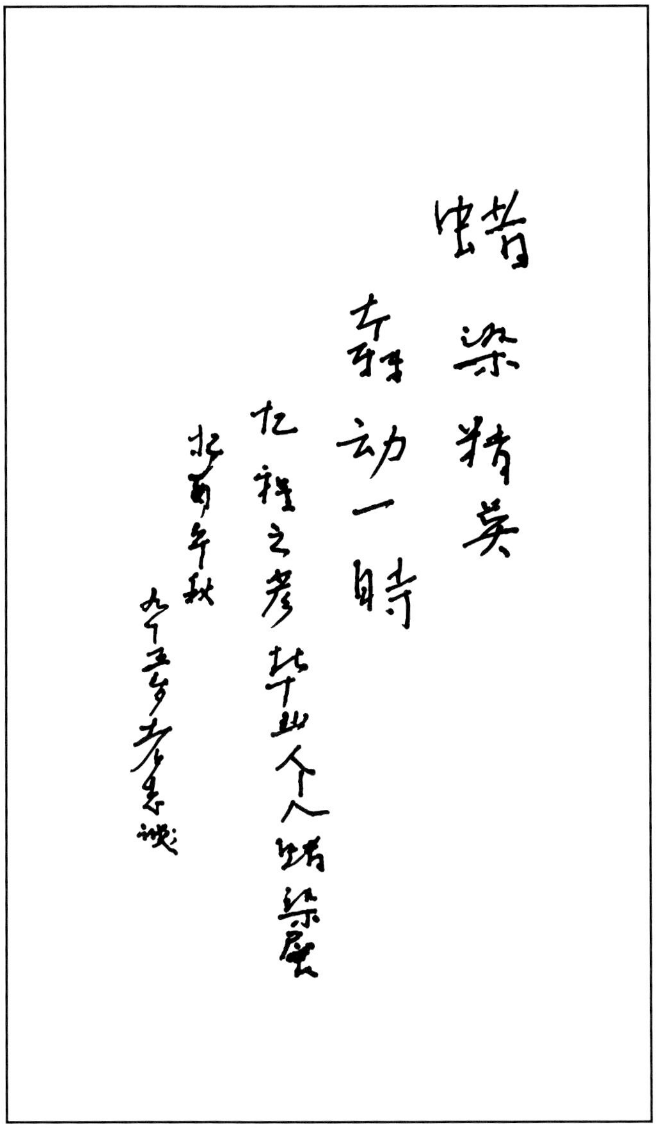

In 2005, world famous pianist and composer Zhicheng Lao, at the age of 95, recalled the special event, "This outstanding batik master created a furor."

世界著名钢琴演奏家、作曲家，九十五岁高龄的老志诚教授， 回忆起当时蜡染画展的盛况，写下:“蜡染精英，轰动一时。忆程之彦毕业个人蜡染展。”

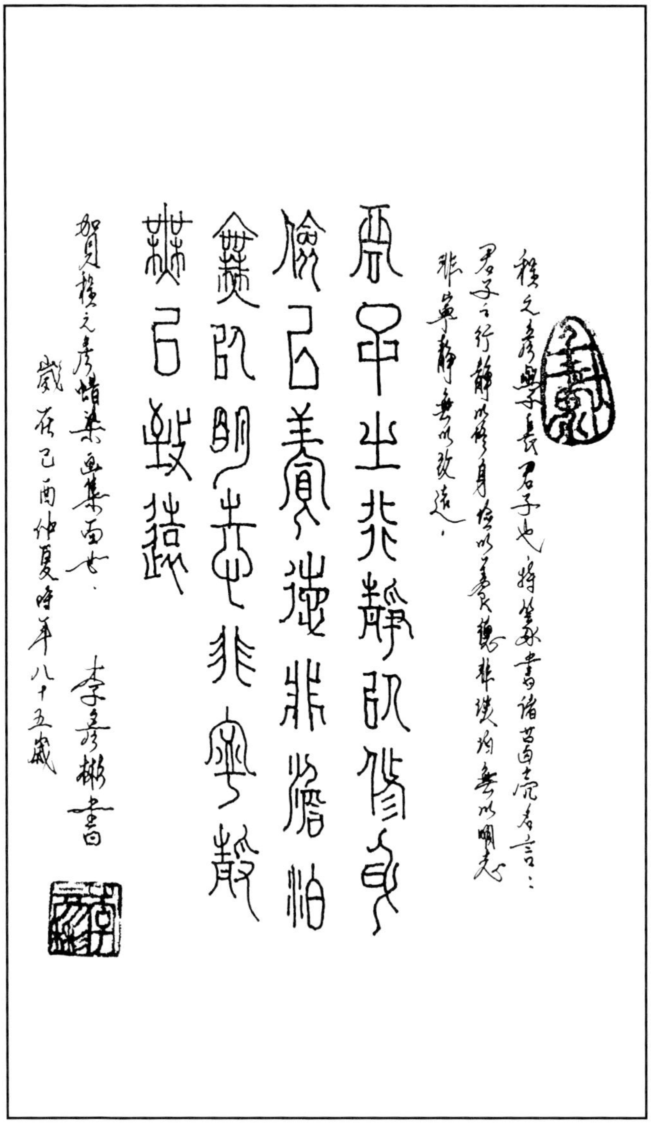

Yanbin Li, Cheng's schoolmate, copied Zhuge Liang's famous "The principal of being a perfect man" in Chinese calligraphy. Li later added, "Cheng met the standard."

程之彦大学同学李彦彬先生，于本画册出版前，借诸葛亮名言，赞许程之彦的为人行事。

Design / Editor: Hsiaoling Cheng
Photographer: Jixiang Wu
Translation: Michael Wu
Proofread: Ziqiang Zhou, Judy Ren
Printed and bound in China
May 2007

美术设计 / 编辑：程小玲
摄影：武吉相
翻译：武岳
中文校对：周自强, 任竹青
印刷：中华商务彩色印刷有限公司
2007 年 5 月

About The Author:

Hsiaoling was born in Beijing and spent most of her early years in China. She graduated from Beijing Tourism Institute in 1982 and went to the United States of America for further studies in 1985 where she received MBA in Finance.

As a child, Hsiaoling was interested in art and calligraphy. She studied calligraphy from the famous Chinese calligraphy master, Zhongxun Tang. Her calligraphy pieces were exhibited many times while she was in college.

She lives in New Jersey with her family and works full-time for a telecommunication corporation. She likes to use her spare time doing many kinds of art activities and is a member of Westfield Art Association in New Jersey. She keeps herself busy attending art shows and enters her father's silk painting pieces in competitions.

作者简介：

程小玲，女，1982 年毕业于北京旅游学院。1985 年赴美深造，获得工商管理(MBA)硕士学位。现任美国一家移动通信公司技术分析师。

自幼喜爱书法和美术。青年时曾师从著名书法家唐仲旬先生学习书法，篆刻。在大学读书期间她的隶书，魏碑等书法作品曾多次参展。赴美深造后定居美国，尽管生活工作十分繁忙，仍利用业余时间参加各项美术活动，并积极为其父程之彦先生举办画展和参加绘画比赛。现任美国新泽西州 WESTFIELD 美术协会会员。